On The Journey

On The Journey

Published by Nancy Kelly

This book contains all original pieces. All writings presented with permission. All scripture is from the King James Version Holy Bible.

Perfect Bound
ISBN 978-1-60416-427-5
Trade Cloth
ISBN 978-1-60416-435-0

Printed On Demand

William's Graphic Design
129 East 5th St.
East Liverpool, OH 43920
1-330 932 0478
Fax 330 932 0478
william@williamgd.com
www.williamgd.com.com

Printed and bound in the United States of America

I have no greater joy than to hear that my children walk in truth.

—3 John 1:4—

Contents

From the Pen of Nancy Kelly

From the Pen of Robert Jackman, Sr.

From the Pen of Ron Jackman

From the Pen of Bob Jackman

From the Pen of Jill Jackman Holler

From the Pen of Others

From the Pen of ...

Nancy Kelly

Think on These Things

When I think upon the goodness of God,
my heart rejoices within.
He chose me one day by His mercy and grace,
and cleansed my heart from sin.
That I might have a hope,
a reason to live,
a purpose to my life,
when at times it seemed that life was filled,
with nothing but trouble and strife.

When you wake in the morning and face the day,
and everything seems to go wrong,
just stop and meditate upon the Lord,
and He'll help you to be strong.
Praise Him for the blessings He's already given,
His grace is sufficient for you.
Think upon good things—not the bad,
upon the pure and the true.

Find someone who is down and out,
and give him a helping hand.
Give a smile to a lonely soul,
it'll make you feel so grand.
Jesus should live on the inside,
He wants to work through you.
You'll soon trade your troubles and your woes
for feelings so grand and true.

So, don't let the devil beat you down,
stand against him and stand against sin.
Remember in the back of the book
my friend, it says that we do win.

This House

When I look out of my windows
and see you looking at me,
I wonder just what you're thinking about
and what do you really see.

Time has taken its toll on my house
and it doesn't look the same.
But that is just a way of life
and there's not a soul you can blame.

Sometimes the back steps creak a bit
and the rafters are turning gray.
The front porch seems to stick out too far
and the siding is beginning to fray.

But, when I look out of my windows
and see you looking my way,
I hope you look as I look and not at
this house made of clay.

For the windows I speak of are not made of glass,
they are the windows of the soul,
and if you look only at the outer man
You're no more than a fool.

The most beautiful person can live
inside the ugliest house, 'tis true,
and the house that is beautiful indeed
might be the house of a shrew.

For if Jesus doesn't live in your soul
and if He doesn't abide,

the sins of this life will tear you down
and make you ugly inside.

But, when He comes into a repentant heart
He does a real good job,
and restores unto you the beauty of life
that Satan would like to rob.

So, when we look at each other
I hope we both will see,
The spirit of Jesus Christ our Lord
living in you and me.

It is in loving—not being loved—
the heart finds its quest;
It is in giving—not in getting—
our lives are blessed.

Free to Fly

If I were a bird,
Oh, how I'd fly,

Up to the uttermost parts of the sky,
Then I'd sweep down to the valley below,

And rest where the cool water doth flow,

Then I'd soar to the mountaintop so high,
Where only is heard the eagle's cry,

But I am a human being you see,

And I must carry this body with me.
A body of flesh with bars of bone,

Which can be unlocked by Jesus alone.

Someday like Jesus, I too will be free,
He'll come and unlock this prison for me.

Then like a mighty bird I'll fly,

Up to the uttermost parts of the sky.

---

*True faith and courage
are like a kite,
An opposing wind only
raises them higher.*

A City of God

I look for a city as Abraham did,
Which has a foundation sure.

A city that none can enter in,
only the holy and pure.

I long for a city not corrupted by man
built on a rock not built on sand.

The light of that city is a precious stone
the Lamb is the light, only He alone.

For He is the Father of all lights,
no shadow of turning to left or right.

They say that the city has streets of pure gold,
and we'll be new and never grow old.

There'll be no more pain or sorrow or woe,
just thinking about it makes me want to go.

When the troubles of this life seem too much to bear
I look up, for my redemption draws near.

Soon Jesus will return in clouds of the sky,
to take His church to be with Him on high.

We'll reign with him in that city so bright,
where nothing is wrong and everything's right.

Come quickly, Lord Jesus, and take us away,
for I can't wait till that glorious day.

A Widow's Prayer

A widow's prayer is full of love,
Also grief and pain.
It's full of emotions rolled up into one,
Because things aren't the same.
When praying for comfort to soothe the soul,
And strength along the way,
Memories flood in like a mighty wave,
Of things of yesterday.
When love was new, and how it grew,
In good times and in bad.
All these things rolled into one,
Something that we had.
If I could once more see your face,
That old familiar smile,
Or touch your hands that worked so hard,
Day after day, mile after mile,
I'd tell you how much I appreciated
The things that you did,
And say all the things that are in my heart,
Words sometimes I hid.
But you are in a better place,
A place of sweet release,
And I'm glad for you and thankful too
For your rest and for your peace.
This earthly path is not finished,
For me I must travel on.
Take my hand Dear Father,
Lead me till life's breath is gone.

Precious Blood

Oh how precious is the blood,
That cleansed me from all sin.
It was a sacrifice of love,
That made me pure within.
The blood was shed upon the cross,
Two thousand years ago,
And through all times and ages,
A crimson stream will flow,
To cleanse the worse of sinners,
To give them life anew.
How many will accept it.
Only a very few.
The blood of God Himself was shed,
Upon that cross that day.
So willingly He shed that blood
To wash our sins away.
With eyes we can not see it,
Through faith we must receive,
That precious blood of Jesus,
Still flows if you believe.

Simple Pleasures

Simple pleasures surround my life,
Relieving me from stress and strife.
Simple pleasures so free to all,
Some are great and some are small.
When I'm down, I look around,
My smile begins to erase the frown.
Hearing the songs of the birds as they fly
To my feeder from the sky.
It's my pleasure to feed the little bird,
God says He sees it. It's in His Word.
Feeling the sun as it warms my face,
And a soft breeze that's here and leaves no trace.
Snowflakes as they drift down,
Painting everything white upon the ground.
Walking through the woods on an autumn day,
The smell in the air of new mown hay.
Watching a hawk circle the sky,
Up, up he goes, so high.
Watching children as they play,
Laughing in their carefree way.
A hug from my grandchild,
That shows I'm loved.
They are a gift from God above.
The conversation between a friend,
A cup of coffee before it ends.
Soft warm blankets upon my bed,
As I lay down and rest my head.
Knowing that God is with me,
All night and all day,
These Simple Pleasures are here to stay.

JESUS KNOWS

Jesus knows the end of a matter,
before it's even begun.
He knows each event that will happen,
from the dawn to the setting sun.

He knows the steps of a righteous man,
his steps are directed by Him.
Sometimes they may slip and falter,
but He cleanses every sin.

He gives the call of repentance,
to every soul on earth,
but already knows
the choice they'll make,
even before their birth.

He knows if they'll accept His plan,
for which His life he gave,
He knows each step a man will take,
from the cradle to the grave.

We can only see through
a glass that is dark,
He sees with vision that's light,
He can guide us on to joys untold,
if we trust in His power and might.

For He is an exceedingly mighty God,
exceeding each deed that He's done.
Awaiting to give us eternal life,
when this race on earth is run.

So, why not put your life in His hands,
letting His will be done,
for Jesus knows the end of a matter,
before it's even begun.

The woods are Nature's Sanctuary

Showing forth the glory of God

Wrapping its beauty and serenity

Around those who wander in.

Come Inside

Come into my side, my spouse,
I hear my Savior say.

I'll keep you from the wrath to come,
there, I'll hide you away.

From Adam's side I took a rib,
and made a bride for him.

Now I'll put back my rib in my side,
a bride that's cleansed from sin.

My side was opened,
when I hung on a tree,
on Calvary's hill one day.

And from it flowed water and blood,
to wash your sins away.

Now it's time to come inside,
and be with me evermore.

For soon, very soon, my lovely bride,
I must shut the door.

For just as I shut the door one day,
upon old Noah's ark,

No one could enter
from that moment on,
they were all lost in the dark.

The name of the Lord is a mighty tower,
and those that come in are safe.

So, be baptized and receive that name,
and be filled with His Spirit and grace.

The Spirit says come,
the bride says come,
Let all that heareth
say come.

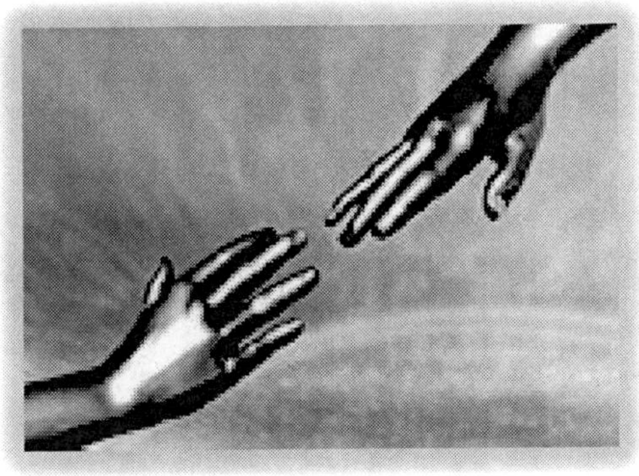

Strength for Today

You've given me strength before,
Dear Lord,
so give it to me today.
I need it so badly, Lord
to help me along the way.

Now, I'm not cold and hungry, Lord,
you've blessed me with more than enough,
but the battle that rages inside of me,
sometimes can get pretty rough.

I know that this is a spiritual war,
that tries to tear me in two,
the devil always trying to win,
help me to make it through.

I know You went through the very same thing,
when You were tempted by him,
but You overcame for You and me,
You escaped without a sin.

Oh Lord, help me to overcome,
give me peace within,
help me to escape this life,
without a spot of sin.

I know the secret of entering in,
to the rest that You have prepared,
it's praising You and thanking You,
and knowing that You've cared.

So, I ask you now to refresh my soul,
with your Spirit from above,
let Your Spirit flow through me,
reassure me with your love.

---

*But, God commendeth His love
toward us, in that
while we were yet sinners,
Christ died for us.*

—Romans 5:8—

My Mother, the Fire Builder

One of my fondest memories of my mother
is her love for building a fire.
She could build a fire when no one else could.
She was very patient,
starting with just a few small pieces of kindling wood
and gradually building to a nice cozy fire.

I can still see her sitting out back in a lawn chair,
an old sweater wrapped around her shoulders,
feet propped up on an old log, and poking at the flames with an old stick.

She was never alone for very long after she built a fire.
One by one we would venture over and pull up a chair and join her.
Sometimes she would call on the phone and say,
"I've got a fire out back, why don't you come over?"
Soon everyone would be there.

The grandchildren were always attracted by the fire
and soon would gather around, too.
She usually had a bag of marshmallows for the kids
and a pot of coffee for the rest of us.
We'd sit there in the warmth of the fire and discuss the events of the day.
We'd reminisce of days gone by, handing down stories
that had been told many times before.
We'd discuss the scriptures from her favorite book, the Bible.
We were a close-knit family that enjoyed being together.

It has been several years now since Mom left us
and somehow the rest of us are not as close as we used to be.

We've gotten all wrapped up in our own little worlds.
Looking back now, I can see how wise she was, and a little bit sly, too.
She knew how to draw us together and keep us close.
She knew how to never be lonely.
She knew how to prevent a generation gap.
The children learned from our conversation.
They learned important values.
They learned important things about our family's past.
They learned history and politics and religious beliefs.
I wonder if she realized what benefits we enjoyed from her little fires.

I miss those nights around the fire.
I think it's about time I start building
some fires of my own.

Joy

Joy is a strange emotion
    It can't be explained, only felt
Like finding an oasis in the desert
    As at the spring of water we knelt
Oh, let our hearts rejoice in this glow
    For as long as it may last
For all too soon the cares of this life
    Will cause this blessing to pass
The joy of the Lord is our strength
    It is declared in His Word
That is why we jump and shout
    When we meet in one accord
The sight of seeing a lost sheep
    Coming back into the fold
Or seeing the Spirit set on fire
    A church that once was cold
The sight of seeing a sinner
    Who is truly repentant of sin
Watching him earnestly striving
    The kingdom to enter in
The thrill of feeling God touch you
    When you're sick or in pain
These joys cannot be matched, my friend
    They are as the refreshing after a rain
People are seeking in the world everyday
    Something to satisfy
But, they'll not find it here on earth
    Until they seek Him on high
If you've not tasted of the joys I speak
    I truly recommend
That you try Jesus in all His truth
    He'll put the Joy within

Asleep in Jesus
In Memory of Thomas Kelly

He lay there, asleep in Jesus
we put a Bible in his hands
a book he read and lived by
just a pilgrim in this land

The Word was his salvation
it brought him eternal life
and now he's with the Lord above
free from pain and strife

He was once a sinner
as you and I were, too
but once he heard the Word of God
he knew what he must do

So, as we put the Bible in his hands
the hands of human clay
we know the Word was in his heart
and now he's gone away

But, we will see him someday soon
he's waiting over there
where Christ will welcome us with love
and wipe away our tears

Draw Nigh to God

Draw night to God
    and He'll draw nigh to you,
this verse in the Bible is oh, so very true.

Sometimes we get so busy
    we forget to pray,
and acknowledge Him who helps us along life's busy way.

Then, we find ourselves all burdened down,
    we seldom smile,
but rather, frown.

We don't feel His Spirit as we should,
    we often think bad thoughts
instead of good.

Oh my, what a fix
    we get ourselves in,
soon we may even start to sin.

But, if we take
    the time each day,
to talk to the Lord along the way,

He'll reach down
    and touch our soul
and give us strength and make us whole.

He's so merciful and knows
    we're only man,
that we often forget to take His hand.

He holds it out to us

each day,
and offers us help along the way.

I thank you, dear Lord,
for the Spirit I feel,
when I bow down and before You kneel.

Help me always to remember this must,
draw nigh to God;
He'll draw nigh to us.

Like a muscle,

Faith must be exercised to be strong.

This is the reason

For the challenges in our lives.

God Loves You

God's love is real, it has always been.
He loved you when He reached down
and saved you from sin.

God came to Earth in the form of a Son,
He had a work of grace to be done.
He preached to the lost and healed the infirm,
a message of love He had to confirm.

Then they beat him with stripes,
He was nailed to a tree.
He did all of this so we could be free.

Free from the power of sin and death,
to live with Him when we take our last breath.
This road of life can get rocky and rough,
but, His love for us is more than enough.

If we have faith and trust in His love,
He'll shine light on our path from up above.
Oh yes, He loves you, and He also loves me.

And His love will go on for eternity.

Jesus Will Fight Your Battles

Before you engage in battle, consider the spoil.
Is it worth your energy, is it worth your toil?
Does it really matter, is it worth your time?
Will it bring you closer to the Lord?
Will the light of the Holy Ghost still shine?
Some battles are better left alone,
They're not important at all.
They only take your mind off God,
And cause you to stumble and fall.
Jesus will fight your battles, if you ask Him to.
The spoil of the battle that He gives,
Is worth it all to you.
If someone says an unkind word,
If something angers you,
Just ask the Lord about it,
He will see you through.
If you can learn to walk away,
And just let it go.
You'll have won the battle,
And your light will also glow.

If God has healed your body...pass it on.

If God has helped you through a trial...pass it on.

If you want to spread the gospel...pass it on.

If you enjoy these words...pass them on.

LOVE

Love is light,
in a world of darkness,
reaching down into the soul.

Love is lifting
the heart that is lonely,
restoring and making it whole.

Love is nurturing;
it is patient and kind,
giving help when needed
to body and mind.

It seeks not its own,
but regards rather others.
It's a world of action
toward sisters and brothers.

They say that actions
speak louder than words,
I know 'tis true,
these words I've heard.

Love is not measured
and cannot be bought,
it is freely given
and eagerly sought.

One who embodies
all the above,
came down to Earth
in the name of love.

He walked this Earth
as you and I,
and after He lived,
He had to die.

He gave His life freely,
He suffered such pain.
He died a death
of anguish and shame.

The third day He arose,
triumphant was He,
that we might have this hope
of eternity.

There is no love greater
than the life He gave,
the hope of resurrection
from the grave.

Autumn's Prayer

Scents of fall are in the air,
the flowers of summer have faded.

Gone are the days of the summer heat
through the long winter days we awaited.

The green leaves of the trees will give way to gold,
shades of red and yellow so bold.

The birds will fly south to a climate that's warm.
We'll stay and endure the cold winter storm.

Another year has gone by
as we ponder the season.
We know in Your will there is a reason.

Give us strength for another year,
we know that Your coming is drawing near.

Help us draw closer as we live each day,
and when it's Your time
just take us away.

The Family Name

Baptized in the name
of Jesus Christ.
Oh, what joy! Eternal life!
Buried with Him in a watery grave,
for this, His life He freely gave,
that we might rise
with newness of life,
burying the old man of sin and strife.
Receiving the blessed name that was given,
to God's family on earth and in Heaven.

Jesus came
in His Father's name,
and the Holy Ghost was sent in the same.
there's power in the name of Jesus Christ,
it can heal and it can give
eternal life.

Someday that name will be shouted on high,
all saints will rise to meet Him in the sky.
So, why not enter this family so blessed,
by taking His name in
water baptism,
so you can have the fullness of life,
through the name of our Savior,
Jesus Christ.

You are a child of God...

...Call home.

Your Friend & Mine

If I could bear your pain,
I would.
It hurts me so
to see you suffer.

I've seen some pain
in my life, as well.
But, now I'm older
and wise.

I've learned in time
the pain will subside,
but, the scar
will always be there.

If you can hold on
and live one day at a time,
the clouds will roll back
and the sun will shine.

I have a friend,
He's your friend, too.
He too, suffered pain
and was falsely accused.

For no reason at all,
He was crucified.
I can only imagine
how He must have cried.

He said we would know Him
by the scars in His hand,
a reminder of pain
inflicted by man.

He knows what it is like,
your pain and mine.
He'll lead you through it
and help you find
strength for each sorrow
and maybe tomorrow,

the sun will shine.

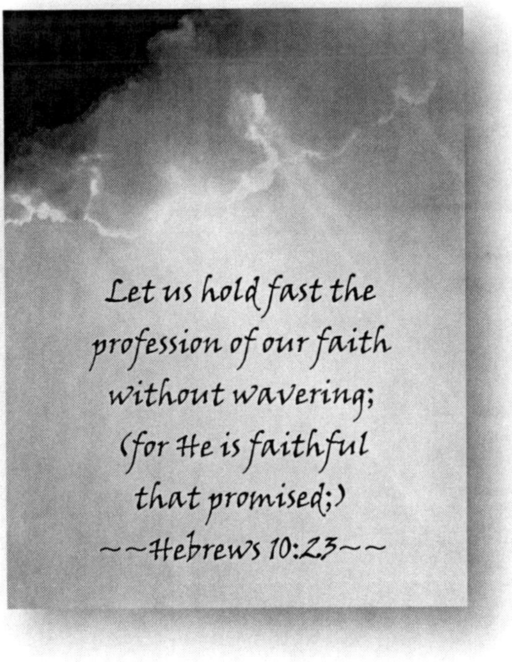

A Little Bit of Faith

I found a little bit of faith
in a faithless land.
I picked it up,
put it in my hand.

It was small,
but I knew it would grow,
for the Bible tells me so.

Seeds of faith
I sowed all around.
Some of them fell
On fertile ground.

A word of hope,
an act of love,
put in my heart
from up above.

Given to me
to share with others.
Those who are lost
and my sisters and brothers.

If you find faith
in a faithless land,
pick it up,
put it in your hand.

The more you share,
the more it will grow
for the Bible tells you so.

He Chose Me

I choose to be with God's people,
because He chose me to be,
before He laid the foundation
of the mighty earth and sea.

I choose to live the life that is holy,
for His Spirit lives in me.
To do His will is my desire,
for His desire was to set me free.

I choose because He chose me,
eternal life's my goal.
There's healing for my body
and redemption for my soul.

I know that life is sometimes hard,
filled with trouble and pain,
but, through the mighty power of prayer,
the sun outshines the rain.

I choose to walk with Him one day,
to see Him face to face,
and thank Him for the blood He shed
and His amazing grace.

From the Pen of...

Robert Jackman, Sr.

Spring Days

My oh my, at last it's spring!
The sun feels hot and
how the birds sing

What could be nicer
than a warm spring day
along Beaver Creek
where the fish
swim and play

I'm just going to sit here
and let the sun's hot rays
burn out all remembrance
of those cold winter days!

Days which I spent
confined in my home
looking out of my window
nowhere to roam

But roam now, I will!
Along creeks and over hills!

I'll smell spring's sweet smells
and forget all my ills

Oh, all the pills in the world
could never make me feel better
than this first breath of spring
which breaks winter's
last fetter!

A Walk in the Woods

I took a walk the other day,
with a problem on my mind.
So full of worldly concentration,
that to nature's beauty I was blind.
The problem went unsolved that day,
and I went on living just the same.
But, to have carried it with me in the woods,
I felt that was a shame.
So, today I took that walk again,
in a different frame of mind.
I left my worldly cares and woes,
yes, my problems too, I left behind.
I found a log upon which I sat,
and began to listen, look and feel.
For my soul, it seemed as though,
it was a full course meal.
The smell of leaves upon damp earth,
a whisper of a breeze,
the noisy hammer of the flicker,
the busy chatter of chickadees,
chipmunks playing their usual game,
of find the man and sound the alarm.
Though the little rascals know, I'm sure,
I wouldn't do them any harm.
Else why would they dare sit on a rock close by,
acting so cocky, staring me right in the eye?

The Woods in Autumn

I like to roam the woods, especially in October,
When leaves are thick upon the ground,
And nature seems so sober.
The little chipmunk and the squirrel
Are storing nuts in hollow trees,
The birds are forming in large flocks,
And south they'll go with the first cold breeze.
October's bright blue weather,
And her beautiful autumn scenes,
If only it could stay that way,
But winter always intervenes.
October seems to spell an end,
To summer's fun and happy times,
It's hard to believe that soon,
We'll hear Christmas music played on chimes.

Photo courtesy of Margaret Holler

From the Pen of...

Ron Jackman

Sabbath of the Sea

Beneath the surface of the ocean,
there's a place serene and free.

It is calm and strangely placid,
called the Sabbath of the sea.

The sea above spits out its fury,
as the tempest rages high.

But, beneath its stormy surface,
such commotions can't come nigh.

In this story, there's an analogy,
when a man is born again.

Though the world around's in turmoil,
there's a joy and peace within.

The Holy Ghost is our comforter,
and from sin has set us free.

In His presence we have sweet repose,
for He's our Sabbath of the sea.

Who is a God like unto thee, that pardoneth iniquity, and passeth by the transgression of the remnant of his heritage? He retaineth not his anger for ever, because he delighteth in mercy. He will turn again, he will have compassion upon us; he will subdue our iniquities; and thou wilt cast all their sins into the depths of the sea.~~Micah 7:18,19~~

And the Word was made flesh, and dwelt among us, (and we beheld his glory, the glory as of the only begotten of the Father,) full of grace and truth.
~~John 1:14~~

And the Word was Made Flesh

To most He was only just a carpenter's son.
Surely, they thought, this man is not the One.
When Messiah was to come,
they knew He'd be a man,
but, where is His army, or where is His band?
They knew that He would come
and walk among men.
Yet this man wore no kingly robe,
or royal diadem.
His kingdom's not an earthly one,
but, is established in men's hearts.
And through His death, burial, and resurrection,
we all can have a part.
Thank God that He has chosen you
thank God He's chosen me.
The hand of God has given light
to His church that we might see.
We understand by the Word of God
that Jesus Christ is His name,
not because we're wise, or rich,
or that we have worldly fame.
It came by revelation through the
ministry God selected.
We are the church triumphant,
we are God's elected.

From the Pen of Ron Jackman

Jesus Christ Our Coming King

If every bell in the world
started ringing,
as a tribute to the King.

If every leader
in our government
paid Him homage in everything.

If every man that hath breath
did praise him
and in prayer did not neglect.

If everything
in God's creation
did bow humbly to show their respect.

All of these things
would be most fitting,
but none of them could repay.

For the ransom He gave
at Calvary
to provide salvation for us today.

By the word of the LORD were the heavens made; and all the host of them by the breath of His mouth.

~~Psalm 33:6~~

He Did it For You and I

One day God stepped out of eternity,
when He spoke all things into place.

In the garden He had made the man Adam,
now God had given His image a face.

The first two in the garden were made perfect,
and of everything, but one tree, could partake.

But, the seed of that old serpent, the devil,
was there waiting for their first mistake.

"If I can get them to taste of the forbidden tree,
the one in the midst of the garden,

"I'll make them believe that they can become gods,
and soon their vain hearts I will harden."

Satan finally thought he had thwarted God's plan,
but a Savior was to come soon after.

He would pay the ransom for that original sin,
and for every transgression committed thereafter.

Jesus Christ paid the price at a terrible cost,
when He took all our sins upon Him.

But He defeated the devil and gave salvation to man,
that day when He hung on the cross.

Things I'm Thankful For

I'm thankful
for the God above
and to know that He is one.

I'm thankful
for such temporal things
like the earth, the moon and sun.

But most of all
I'm thankful
for His tender love for me
and for the precious blood He shed
on the mount called Calvary.

So if you want salvation,
then I say, please take the time
to search out one scripture
Acts 2:38
as noted in this rhyme.

Of salvation there is no other,
so take heed without delay.
It worked for those of the early church,
and it works for us today.

I'm thankful
that I tried it,
and have forgiveness
from my sins,
and now I sing
a joyful song
for now I've been
born again.

A True Story

There was a man
where I worked
    whose name was Fred.

He was preached
the gospel
    but, chose the world instead.

I opened the Bible
and to him
    the scriptures read.

But the gospel never
seemed to enter
    into Fred's head.

He fussed and
rejected and by
    peer pressure was led.

Till the day he died
one lonely night
    on his bed.

So, now I am thinking
there's nothing
    in Fred's head.

For the dead know
nothing, and now
    Fred is dead.

The Skating Pond

As is sit here reminiscing about days of long ago,
I can almost hear the northern winds and see the drifting snow.
And if I close my eyelids, a picture comes to mind,
Of skating ponds and childhood friends, and as my thoughts unwind,
I hear again our laughter as we glided o'er the ice,
And even hear our neighbors call to join them on the ice.
Upon the bank we'd build a fire, all cozy warm and bright,
For all the neighbors and the kids to warm their hands just right.
The smell of burnt rubber sometimes filled the air,
From someone who got too close and didn't take good care.
The aroma of wood smoke, kerosene, soft light,
And finally, childish voices, echoing songs into the night.
And then it all was over, and we turned our faces toward home,
With a memory tucked inside our hearts to recall where ere we roam.

Directions We Must Travel

If a man flatters you with the tongue, then
Look out.
If you are criticized of a fault, then
Look in.
If you are forsaken by your friends, then
Look up.
If you are riding on your high horse, then
Come down.
If you are at the river of despair, then
Cross over.
If you have left off following truth, then
Come back.

The Man I Used to Be

Sometimes a ghostly stranger walks the hallways of my mind.
It seems that I should know him, from a distance far behind.
His presence is just a memory, of the way it used to be.
Of one who walked in darkness, for the light he could not see.
Sometimes his aimless wanderings, comes a-knocking at my door,
But since that I've been born again, I walk with him no more.
I don't really mind his presence there, for he cannot bother me,
It is there for just one purpose, to remind me of a man.
A man who walked in darkness, the man I used to be.

And the Spirit and the bride say, Come.

And let him that heareth say, Come.

And let him that is athirst, Come.

And whosoever will,

Let him take the water of life freely.

~~Revelation 22:17~~

In Memory of Gerald Holler

There are many in this way, I'm sure
who can really talk the talk.
But, very few with firm conviction,
who can daily walk the walk.

I've heard preachers by the dozens,
who could adroitly expound the Word,
but not so many, I do believe,
who by example could be heard.

I would rather see a living testimony
than to hear one anyway.
And this is what our brother did,
as he walked it day by day.

Your presence will be missed today,
by family and by friends.
As your earthly temple returns to dust,
your spirit will God attend.

May I see you in glory,

Brother Gerald Holler

Missed by Many

Loved by All

The Wonder of It All

When I consider
the smallest atom
to the heavens' great expanse,
I wonder how an intelligent man could say
it happened all by chance.

They grope in the dark
like blind men
to find answers to it all,
but the Word of God gives the answers
from the greatest to the small.

I'm thankful God's Spirit abides in me,
the One that put all things in place,
and it didn't take two billion years my friend,
it only took six days.

God's greatness goes beyond our thinking,
we cannot yet comprehend,
but when He returns we'll understand
for Jesus Christ
is the beginning and the end.

The Many Ways We Pray

Some feel that it's most fitting
to pray upon your knees,
While others deem it proper
with eyes closed so you can't see.

Many clasp their hands together
and bow their heads down to the ground.
But of all the ways that you can pray,
there's another I have found.

There was this man, a Mr. Hurd,
who fell headfirst down a well.
He cried aloud to God above,
as he hung there quite a spell.

So if you were to inquire
as to how that you should pray,
just go to the man who hung upside down
and I'm sure that he would say

"If you really want to touch the Lord,"
says the grateful Mr. Hurd,
"do it with your head straight down
and your toes pointing straight upward."

So the moral to this story
is as evident from the start,
it matters little the position of the body
but the position of the heart.

The Tongue

Oh, little member
how harmless you look.
Lying concealed
in your dark little nook.
I've heard many stories
of the things you do.
I've witnessed the evidence,
so believe they are true.
How strange such a one
that can maim and can kill,
has also the power
to bind and to heal.
Unusual indeed is
the place where you stay.
Behind bars sealed tightly
to shut out the day.
Your place like a prison
has bars you don't see.
But the one difference is,
your place has no key.
The bars they come open,
and they at your will,
once loosed you go searching
for ears you might fill.
Lord, those that are chosen,
may I be among.
Be merciful dear Jesus to me,
a tongue.

And he hath on his vesture and on his thigh a name written, KING OF KINGS, AND LORD OF LORDS.

~~Revelation 19:16~~

The King is Coming

I'm not rich, well known or famous
    Yet, I'm a child of a well known King.

My riches lie in heavenly places,
    And not in earthly things.

My needs He knows and will supply
    According to His riches in glory.

So by faith I trust and do believe
    In the promises He has for me.

Return He will to earth again,
    To gather up His bride.

And in His everlasting arms we'll stay,
    Forever to abide.

Jesus Christ is that King of Kings,
    And He's coming back real soon.

So make your final preparations church,
    To meet the coming groom.

The Idler's Chair

It's when we sit in idleness
that Satan attacks us there.
When we get real lax and comfy
as we sit in the idler's chair.
But, when we come together to hear
God's Word and do what's right,
you'll find the devil can't take the heat
and for now he'll take his flight.
But return again, he will real soon
and when you least expect,
to try and weaken or destroy
the Faith of God's elect.
So, put on now God's Armor
with His Gospel shoes be shod,
that the imprint of God's message
be left in places they have trod.
So, be faithful in God's service
as you labor day by day,
and take heed unto the ministry
and to the words that He might say.
So, what you hear, do practice,
be obedient and don't balk.
For as you sit and listen,
you shall also learn to walk.
The words of which I've spoken
are a warning, but don't despair,
for God is simply telling us
don't sit in the idler's chair.

Hope for Our Children

Sometimes it's hard to feel positive,
while living in this negative world.

For down here it's Satan's kingdom,
as his banner of sin is unfurled.

He struts about going to and fro,
seeking whom he may devour.

He ensnares the young at the early age,
as they play in the idle hour.

So, saints this message I pass on to you,
as the preacher man gave it to me.

Train up your child in the way they should go,
they'll not depart from this truth, you will see.

For, as they grow older and wiser,
soon conviction will tire them of sin.

And one glorious day unexpected,
they'll return to this truth once again.

As It Is Written

Don't make attempts
to change God's Word
not even just a little.

For none of it shall pass away,
not one jot nor one tittle.
There are warnings in the Word of God,
to any who have meddled.

For His Words are pure and undefiled,
and in heaven they are settled.
The Church of God, down through the years,
on its precepts they have stood.

I would not change one word of it,
even if I could.

No adding or subtracting
with intentions to deceive,
for if we add unto His Words,
His plagues we shall receive.

So, take a stand upon His Word,
and the critics do forbear.

For in the Lamb's Book of Life,
our names are written there.

The Love of God

You can search the whole world over,
sift through every grain of sand.

Search through the halls of ivy,
throughout this wondrous land.

Turn over every mossy rock
and search the depths of the murky seas.

There you will not find the love of God,
for He's found in none of these.

God's love is freely given
and it reached down for you and me.

It transcends the bonds of time and space,
it's something you can't see.

But, if you humbly bow your heart,
and call upon His name.

He'll fill that empty place in you,
and you'll never be the same.

God's Arithmetic

One + One + One = One

You ask a man if there is a God,
and some say there isn't any.
The church world says that there are three,
but I find that's too many.

The Bible says there is the Father,
the Holy Ghost and Son,
but if you read it carefully,
it says these three are one.

Your carnal mind will reason,
but you'll always say there are three.
So until you're filled with the Holy Ghost,
just leave this mystery be.

It comes only by God's Spirit
and by obedience to His Word.
And once you have received it,
the trinity will seem absurd.

One Lord, one faith and one baptism
that's all there is my friend.
His Holy Word declares it,
right to the very end.

So, if you want this revelation,
I find it's not too late,
to bow your knee to the Word of God
and obey Acts 2:38.

There is one body, and one Spirit, even as ye are called in one hope of your calling; One Lord, one faith, one baptism, One God and Father of all, who is above all, and through all, and in you all.

~~Ephesians 4:4-6~~

Are You Bound

When the call is made to worship
and we gather in one place,
the devil also comes this day
to find some empty space.
He comes into the meeting
and he stealthily walks around,
to find some weakened vessels
so that worship might be bound.
So, if you're ever in a meeting
where he's wandering about,
just take a stance in Jesus' name
and in His name just shout,
I have got the victory and in His name
I'm free!
And all the things you stand for
you'll find, I disagree.
So, if you've come amongst us,
to put our service down
just look below, I've made a list
of the many ways I'm bound.
I was bound to come to church today,
to offer up His praise,
and I'm bound to serve Him faithfully
and acknowledge all His ways.
I'm bound to love the Lord today,
and have love one to another.
I am bound to know one God,
you see for a Savior there is no other.
So, in the name of Jesus Christ, today
I command you, "take your leave."
For a saint who is word-taught and
blood-bought, you'll find you can't deceive!

And as you might suspect by now
we're already bound,
    we're bound to serve the Lord.

The Rescue Ship

Has your vessel's worth been tested
on the open seas of life
Has its worthiness been proven
through the storms of stress and strife.

Some ships never leave the harbor
safely anchored and secure
Not knowing if they're seaworthy
for they've never left the shore.

The clarion call for us today is
launch out into the deep
Let down your nets to catch the draught
be vigilant lest you sleep

The work is not done in the harbor,
but rather the open sea
For there are many adrift whom God has said,
there are some who belong to Me.

Almost Persuaded

Almost thou persuadeth me,
and at a more convenient season,
Were statements in the book of Acts,
deduced by human reason.

Festus and Agrippa let time
sadly pass them by,
for at their time of visitation,
God's salvation they did deny.

For by the ticking of the clock of time,
from which we cannot borrow,
Seek the Lord while He can be found,
boast not thyself of tomorrow.

Oh, that men from everywhere,
could repent and see their need,
And by the urging of the Holy Ghost,
their spirit would take heed.

For how fickle is the time we travel,
and how quickly it skips on by,
So, when God's spirit to you does beckon,
may His grace you not deny.

You can accomplish more in hour with God, than one lifetime without Him.

THE GREAT ESCAPE

If only I could get beyond
the confinement of these walls.

If I could walk right through those gates
and escape these dismal halls.

I would give one leap of exaltation
and shout, "At last I'm free!"

For from this prison of my flesh
now I have liberty.

I read one time in the book of the prophets
of One who was to come.

He opened up the prison doors and gave
a song to the lips of the dumb.

One day He loosed me from this prison,
as the gates flung open wide.

I now have joy and peace within,
through the opening in His side.

He brought me out and took me in,
now forever to abide.

I now not only have peace with God,
but a piece of Him within.

For, now I am walking in a new direction,
as I've turned from where I've been.

Pressing Onward

If a man can learn from his past mistakes,
then looking back is not in vain.

But, to stew and worry about those by-gone days,
brings only discouragement, hurt and pain.

But, one sweet day, God took away
those things that troubled me.

For the things back then are cast away,
and by His grace I am now set free.

He gave me a peek beyond the veil,
and a hope that spurs me on.

My affections are not set
on temporal things.

But on things
that are beyond.

From the Pen of...

Bob Jackman

Pass Away

I stopped along the way and looked up and thought, Oh Lord I miss my mother and my dad and the times gone by. But something seemed to say, these things must pass away, pass away, pass away.

Even my brother and my sister and the walks we had along the creeks and through the woods: But these things must pass away, pass away, pass away.

My children are now all grown and from the nest they have flown: But these things also must pass away, pass away, pass away.

I stood and looked upon a big red oak tree, and admired its huge trunk and gigantic limbs. I thought of the many generations it had seen come and go and the tales it could tell if it could only speak: But this too must pass away, pass away, pass away.

God's Word says that life is brief and that we spend our years as a tale that is told. It's like a vapor, it appeareth for a little while and then vanisheth away.

I must be moving on now, for I too someday must pass away, pass away, pass away.

From the Pen of...

Jill Jackman Holler

Traveling Shoes

These old shoes of mine, I think are wearing thin.
The heels are flat, and the cold air gets in.
But they've taken me to places I've wanted to go,
And I know that they will last 'til I get home.

These shoes have taken me
across some rocky shores,
Down some valleys and through
a lot of bitter storms.
Sometimes they look like they
will tear,
But I know Jesus will give me a
brand new pair.
Sometimes I think I'm walking
all alone,
And I wonder how much more I
have to go on.
But I know if I keep walking,
someday I'll find,
Jesus walking beside me with shoes like mine.
These are my traveling shoes, that I got on.
I've walked many miles and I've seen how far I've come.
And I know I'll see Jesus very soon,
And I'll thank Him for these traveling shoes.

My Father and I

As a child, my father and I would go on many walks,
Up hills and through streams,
And along old railroad tracks.
The questions I would ask as we would
Walk on those trails.
Oh, the wisdom as he spoke of many a tale.
He spoke of the times of his own childhood days,
And of walks with his father just like this he would say.
I watched so carefully each footstep he walked.
If I could put my feet in his prints, oh, how I thought,
For he didn't slip so neither shall I.
On these walks with my father, just him and I,
I thought of my heavenly Father,
And the many steps He took.
If I can just walk where He walked,
And stand where He stood,
Oh the joy and perfection and great gain I shall find,
As I walk with my Father, just Him and I.

Great is Thy Faithfulness

When we aren't faithful, He is still faithful.
When we leave Him, He never leaves us.
He would never leave us nor forsake us.
When we were unforgiving, He forgave.
When we were nowhere to be found,
He was very present.
When we were guilty, He was blameless.
When we were weak, He was strong.
His strength is made perfect in our weakness.
When we meant it for evil, He meant it for good.
When we were afraid, He was peace.
When we were oppressed, He was hope.
When we were in darkness, He was light.
When we were strangers, He was our near kinsman.
When we were sick, He was health.
When we were dead in sin, He was life more abundant.
When we were without mercy, He was merciful.
His mercies are new everyday.
When we were forgetful, He was mindful of us.
When we were broken, He molded us again.
When we were in much sorrow,
He gave us the oil of gladness.
Truly without Him we are nothing and can do nothing.
For in Him we move and breathe and have our being.
Thank you, Lord, for being all in all to me.

Remembering

As I look back through the years, my memory starts to
unfold,
Of the precious times of childhood days that's so dear to my
soul.
I can remember times of family, of laughter, and of fun,
And wishing I could go back right now to those days when I
was young.
And as I think and ponder of those wonderful days gone by,
I always try to keep in touch with my family ties.
For it's not until you're grown and from your family you
depart,
Do you realize how precious they are and so dear to your
heart.
And although I am apart from my family so far away,
The miles will never take from me the memories I cherish
each day.

Teach Me Lord

Teach me to live Lord, in Your perfect will each day.
Put a right Spirit within me, that I may grow in the way.
You know how weak I really am,
For You created me flesh, just simple man.
But one day You saw that I needed help from above,
So You left Your throne in glory and came down in love.
You died and shed Your blood for my sins,
But after three days You arose and now live again.
Then You put in me a part of Your Spirit to dwell,
So that my soul would no longer be bound for hell.
I'm so glad You made me this new creature in You,
Without your Spirit the flesh would do what it wanted to do.
So that is why I pray this prayer each day,
Teach me to live, Lord, and walk in Your way.

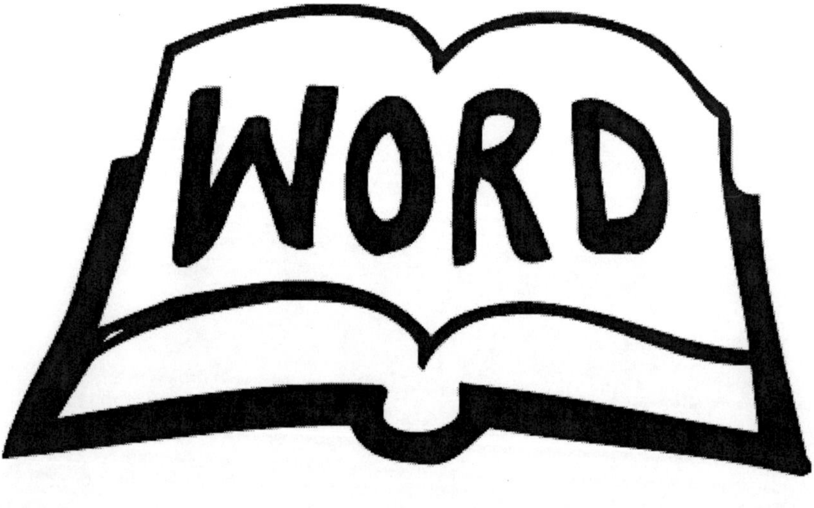

From the Pen...

of Others

Lonesome Traveler

Like a traveler to a land who hears the stories oh so grand
The sights are wondrous, the air is pure,
How you would wish that time was no more.
So you go, these wonders to see.
You leave your friends, your family.
As you gaze at what you found,
You turn and look around,
Only to find no one to share,
For you have left the ones that care.

Thomas Andrew Kelly

For God so loved the world, that He gave His

Only begotten

Son, that whosever believeth in Him should not

Perish, but have

Everlasting

Life.

John 3:16

GOSPEL (Good News)

My Dad

My dad taught me so many things in this life
In his own quiet way he struggled for what was right.
He taught me to love my enemies even if they were wrong.
He taught me to hold my peace and to be strong.
At the drop of a hat he would do for a stranger,
To help them out if they were ever in danger.
My dad was the greatest man that I know,
I only wish he could've watched his grandson grow.
Someday I pray my son will be like him,
Hardworking and loving with that silly grin.
I know it will be a while before I see his face,
Till we meet again, Dad, by God's grace!
I love you and miss you, Dad.

Love, Megan Kelly Stokes

Too Soon

She starts school today.
Seems like she was born the other day.
Learning how to read and write,
Like a baby bird taking flight.
All the new friends she will make,
I hope they're real and not fake.
I watch her get on the bus,
So proud and without a fuss.
Don't worry, she'll be back at noon.
My heart still breaks because it's
All too soon.

Ben Kelly

I Too, Lord

As the cats in the jungle cry out at night
I too, Lord, cry out for You.
As the wind sways, rocking the trees,
I too, Lord want to feel the warmth of Your touch.
As the rose blooms with the morning light,
I too, Lord, want to awake with You guiding me.
As the dew glitters upon the dawn's grass,
I too, Lord, want to be a sparkle in Your eyes.
As the oyster holds its pearl within,
I too, Lord, want a resting place within You.
As the stars shine in the evening sky,
I too, Lord, want You to shine in my mind.
As the thunder chases the lightning flash,
I too, Lord, want to follow You.
As the planets journey around the sun,
I too, Lord, would travel great lengths to be with You.
As the mother keeps her child at close bond,
I too, Lord, love You forever.

Penny Kelly
1970-2005

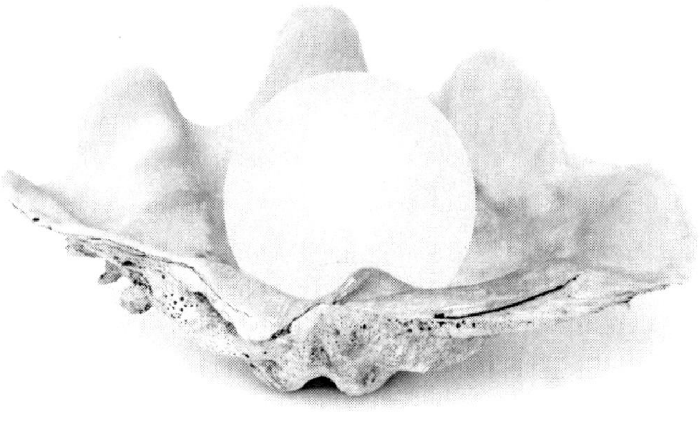

JEREMY

The quiet spirit you wore through your life,
Is what we cling dear to through sorrowful nights.
Your laughter and smile,
Your sweet gentle ways,
Will stay with us always,
They never will fade.
Our tears that have fallen
Like rain from above,
Are each one a memory,
Of you we so loved.
Heartache and sorrow,
No more will they test.
May God's peace surround you,
And give you sweet rest.

Annette Kelly Boyd

A Song for Jeremy

You'll always have a place in my heart.
I can still hear your voice,
Though it seems so far away.
But when I think of you,
I fight so hard to chase them all away,
These tears.
Are you still the same
Such a kind-hearted man,
But still the boy in my dreams?
From those memories,
I will not let them fade,
For one more day,
So much misery,
I cannot understand,
Why you left.
Now your pain is gone,
But mine has just begun.
I'll miss you till the end.

His Brother, Neil Boyd

CALEY'S FIRST BIRTHDAY

When I looked into your eyes and saw you staring back at me,
I couldn't help but feel all the love you bring.
When I took you in my arms and held you close to me,
My heart felt it was finally free.
If I had the world to give, I wouldn't hesitate,
I'd give it all to you.
If I had to live my life again,
I'd do it all the same, I wouldn't change a thing.
Like an angel, you arrived,
And taught me there was much to see.
Before you were here there was nothing to me.
You took me by surprise, and gave your little heart to me.
Now I feel I can finally breathe.
If I had the world to give, I'd give it all to you.
If I had to live my life again, I'd do it all the same,
I wouldn't change a thing.

Her dad, Caleb Boyd

Printed in the United States
149554LV00002B/1/P